A Beginner's Guide to Heaven

Poems by

Jennifer Clark

A Beginner's Guide to Heaven

Poems by

Jennifer Clark

A Beginner's Guide to Heaven
Copyright © 2019 Jennifer Clark
All Rights Reserved.

Published by Unsolicited Press
Portland, Oregon
(503) 864-6533
info@unsolicitedpress.com
www.unsolicitedpress.com

No part of this book may be reproduced or transmitted in any form or by any means without written permission from the publisher or author.

Unsolicited Press Books are distributed by Ingram.
Printed in the United States of America.

Attention schools and businesses: for discounted copies on large orders, please contact the publisher directly.

Cover Art: Elizabeth Patterson
Editor: S.R. Stewart; Kristen Gustafson

ISBN: 978-1-947021-44-0

Contents

I. In the Beginning
   The World Singing   13
   Storming Versailles   18
   Field Guide to Widows and Crows   19
   The Ecology of Fear   21
   Fourth Grade Place Settings   22
   Overture to the Porch on Crane Avenue   24
   A Beginner's Guide to Heaven   26
   The Hebrew Bible Concerns Itself with the Movement of Birds   29
   A Concise History of Michigan Cartology   30
   Grieving the God of My Youth   31
   Cruddy Knees   34
   The Trouble with Reading In Your Hometown   37
   Like the Parents They Never Knew   38

II: The Holy Family
   Castaways   42
   Maestro   43
   Psoriasis Siren   44
   Optimal Foraging Theory   46
   The Great Shrinking Scare of 1985   48
   The Succulent Ones   49
   The Word Whoreder   50
   As Saturn Turns   52
   Sending the Dogs Off   54
   Small Prayer for Margaret   56
   They played Brady Bunch on Saturdays   58

Searching	59
Subpoenaing the Dead	60
Having Bought St. Joseph, I Bury Him	61
Sriracha: Sultan of Sauce	64
Back when hair bows were in fashion	66
Sketch of life form at library	67
The House that Jack Built	69
Cotton Candy Lady, Corner of Fifth & Wood	71
World's Greatest Extra	72
She Stops Seeing Her Beauty at Age Seven	73
Zombie Mommy	75
To all the B saints	77
Lists	78

III. In the Meantime

Waiting and Entering	82
Remember When Corn Was Corn	83
Autotomy, Self-Amputation	85
She Was His Favorite Chapter	86
I Want a Church	88
Winter Kudzu of Kalamazoo	90
On Good Friday, Walmart Wants to Save You	91
What We Do With Our Stuff	93
How to Become a Virgin	95
Protecting the Boys	96
If You Could Stand on Saturn	97
Magnetic Findings in the Czech Republic	99
What We Don't Tell Our School Volunteers	101
Upon Reading the Settlement Agreement in Re: to Lyondell Chemical Company, *et al.*,	103
Doctrine on the Primacy and Infallibility of Digital	

Billboards and Such	105
Obsession #248: Moths	108
Dandelions	109
Longing for the Dynamite Days	111
Oberon, rock the ground whereon these sleepers be	113
A Bad Feminist Reads the Bible	115
God of Plum and Thistle	117
Acknowledgements & Notes	119
About the Author	123

To Bob and Mary,
   two of the best heaven-makers I know.

I. In the Beginning

The World Singing

i. Violins

We are but
stringed instruments
playing to time,

slipping through
hourglass shapes,
all its varnished parts

neck, bridge,
chinrest, tailpiece
and yes,

f-holes,
quaking, trilling
wearing away

until all that sings
is silver.

ii. The Singing Penis

The water boatman, an insect
the size of a grain of rice,
nine eyelashes or less,

sings by rubbing

his wisp of a penis
against his belly, like

drawing bow to moon
he fiddles around,
a microscopic crooning.

Is every
thing dependent
upon length

and tension
of string?
Somewhere,

a finger
presses
down,

engenders
sharp
sounds.

iii. Wood

We wonder why
the Stradivarius
sings so.

Credit the voice of angels
to a mix of craft and
climactic cooling.

Trees
grew slowly,
ring upon huddled ring

bundled in
bathrobes of bark
against Europe's cold spell,

long forgotten
mini-ice age that
peaked in 1643, thawed

enough so that one
year later, the tight
lips of Anna Stradivari

opened, and Antonio
slipped into the cold world
and cried.

When he was old enough,
he took a knife
and, as London burned,

carved from a
block of wood
his first of a thousand

fiddles.

350 years later,
600 remain,
offering up

silky
sounds
hinting

at caramel.

iv. Fungus

You want it, again and again,
will go to great lengths to
reconstruct that first time

you heard it, even if it means
clawing damp earth with bare hands
to perfect the way sound travels
through wood at just the right speed.

This too is an art: to find a loamy forest,
dig up just the right gilled mushrooms,
rub well into slabs of spruce or massage
slowly into maple. Impregnate it.

Allow fungi to grow and rob just
the right amount of beauty, until
it is a masterpiece of decomposition.
Take proper care.

Permit the body,
a fragile instrument in need of rest,
to lie gently upon a clean, cotton sheet,

and with silt already asleep, curled under beds
of fingernails, stretch out as one magnificent string.

Storming Versailles

Sometimes a woman must march thirteen miles in rain,
ruin her only shoes for a slice of bread.

Because justice is not a whispered thing, she and her 6,000 sisters
refuse to yield pitchforks, pikes, and swords.

Even after the royal family flees the palace, the noblemen,
bent on picking every last crumb for themselves,

will swipe at the women's harvest, call them
cross-dressing whores—a small price to pay for flour.

Field Guide to Widows and Crows

Identification
Large bodied, cloaked in night. Emits, at times, a loud cry,
like wind howling across a cavernous well.
Indistinct from each other save by the flash of finger;
the widow parting with her last precious mite.
The study of widowhood is deeply gendered, with a
lack of interest in observing males because
(a.) they do not last long in the wild and
(b.) are well-suited to patriarchal landscape
(see *Widowhood: Condition or Construction*).
Unfortunate categorizations of lusty, scheming,
merry, and virtuous persist to this day.

Range
They are found in the foothills
of the Rockies and elsewhere. Several flocks
established convents throughout Spain. Though
widows rarely fly across borders, both
are widely distributed across all hemispheres.

Habitat
Typically do best where food is prevalent.
Found near woods, beaches, and open fields,
they glean crops of casserole and corn. Some are
forced to eat meat at tables of kindly neighbors.
Can adapt to loss of mate and loud noises.
To understand impact of flux in land-use patterns
and habitat loss, further study required.

Behavior
Highly intelligent creatures (how often have you seen
either species splayed roadside?), they survive by wit.
Easily irritated, they brood for a time. Most move on.
Both benefit from presence of a sentinel. Reports indicate
widows have grown less wary.

Legal Status
Whereas, for thousands of years, open season has been declared
on widows, crows are protected by the Migratory Bird Treaty Act
unless found "committing depredations upon ornamental trees
or when concentrated in such numbers to constitute a health
hazard or nuisance."

Widow management
Wear brightly colored clothes in any abatement
method. Also note, thinning of trees by one-third
does not dislodge offending widows. A combination
of wooing and fright tactics are most effective. (For details,
see *So You've Got a Widow/Crow Problem?*) Be on the lookout
as both species tend to return to their original roosting site.
Even if considered a nuisance, dispersal of widows is not advised.

The Ecology of Fear

Bare legged stems
dangle from mouths

of grazers on the move
who, sensing something

is not right, cease chewing,
listen and look back.

Not out of nostalgia
        but fear:

they might be next—
      culled from their herd

by a hungry wolf or bear.
          They move on.

The vigilant survive.
    Saplings of balsam fir

live to tell
    the understory.

Fourth Grade Place Settings

Lunchtime is out of hand, children, Principal Sister Josephine shouts, stabbing a fork in the air. *You have made a mockery of this school, wasted precious money ruining these forks. This childish behavior will stop immediately.*

The only thing that seems out of hand is Sister Josephine, all red-faced, piercing nothing but air with a droopy-looking fork. I realize, for the first time, nuns have breasts. Each time Sister Josephine inhales, Jesus, on his shiny cross rises. She exhales and he falls. *Nuns are brides of Christ,* Sister Josephine once told us. Sister is married to Jesus and he is always with her, rising and falling with the tremendous tide of her bosom.

I wonder what it feels like to be Sister Josephine's husband, surfing on the edge of her world, arms outstretched, rising over a sea of startled faces as the hot wind of wife rushes down his spine. I feel badly for Jesus. He is a good husband, always there for her, riding her every breath. He must be tired of her yelling. It's too bad she seems to have forgotten him. If Sister Josephine hadn't leashed Jesus to her neck he could jump off and sit at our lunch table. I'd offer him a bite of carrot or peanut butter and honey sandwich and he could rest his arm around Danny Fremont who is crying and tell Danny not to be afraid of his roaring wife. Jesus rises.
Then falls.

The next day, we eat our lunch, gaping at the cafeteria's bulletin board. Peace has disappeared, the cardboard flowers and doves replaced with mangled utensils. Whoever did this was determined. It had to have taken some doing to get silverware wired to the board.

Sister Josephine marches past my table and I feel myself shrinking. Sister's husband looks even smaller today, just a shiny, trembling crumb of man. *This is what you have done*, snaps Sister Josephine, standing before the gallery of forks, tines curled in disgust. *I hope you are pleased with yourselves. The next child I catch bending our silverware—*

It never occurred to me that I have the power to bend metal. Holding a spoon between the table and my stomach, I press into it. Sister Josephine drones on. My spoon thrusts back its shiny head and laughs.

Overture to the Porch on Crane Avenue

She has been here
even before
the beginning of you,
a wall flower of sorts.

Veiled in mist,
atop Westnedge Hill,
she gazes down
upon Kalamazoo in full swing.

You have loved her your entire life,
this grand dame. Her regal frame,
gowned in a spindled skirt
curves like a crescent moon
'round clapboard hips.

Longing to be lifted off your feet
you imagine calling upon her,
climbing the sweep of stairs, that lovely
train that beckons you to promenade,

but your timing is off—
she is already taken.
You allow for proper distance
and waltz on by.

In all seasons, though,
you can't help but come back to her,
smitten by her rounded rhythm,

her generous place of pause.

When wet notes fall from the sky
damp children run to her. She harbors them,
takes in stride their clumsy footwork,
creaks contentedly as they
stomp about, then enter the mystery

of her through a boned bodice.
The world is beating.
You soft-shoe it home.

Later, when tempo slows,
out of the corner of your eye
you will see her shivering,
a flimsy shawl of snow
blanketing her feet.

You will keep walking.

A Beginner's Guide to Heaven

I. It is Close.

I was driving
somewhere
the car slicing us
through fog that had settled
on spines of trees

and dragged
its moist tongue
across the stretch of road
the whole world
steaming

when, from behind,
towering in his car seat
my son said,
*This world is closer
than you think.*

II. Do Not Look Up.

Do you imagine
slogging below this sky
heavy with dead
aunts and uncles,
all those great-greats

who gallop to harps
on coalesced clouds?
Gathered together,
they taste
the divine spread

and toast
their good fortune
having made it
to the feast.
Roaring like thunder

they carry on without us—
the beggars below
this great banquet
blinded by
crumbs.

III. It is Here.

The makings
of holy
are right
here
at our feet

where we
stumble
over tools
strewn
carelessly
where, even
in our

foggy state,
they linger
for us.

Do not wait
to be worthy,
just pick
one.

Roll up
your sleeves
while we
still have time
to build.

The Hebrew Bible Concerns Itself With the Movement of Birds

In the Sinai Desert
Israelites wondered in wilderness
why they ever left home—
at least slavery was something known.

Were it not for migrating quail,
they might have been seduced
by the false god of going-it-alone.

They cast eyes upwards, cease their mutterings
as coveys of quail shamble down from the sky.

Ungainly creatures, their stout bodies transform
into a circle, tails in the center.

Nestled neighbor next to exhausted neighbor,
hundreds of eyes peer out in all directions.

A solid ring now, they sleep, rekindling
hope—that holy soup of seeking.

We forage together.
Let us curl up in morning dew
with the Divine. Then rise.

A Concise History of Michigan Cartology

When someone asks where we live, we
without pause, hold up our right hand

mitten-style, so that the asker can survey
as we press finger to flesh.

Right here, we say. *I grew up right here.*
We carry history on our hands.

Cartographic handlers of hope
and place, our maps swing at our sides

slipped into pockets, folded, laced or
curled until someone asks for directions,

inquires as to where we are going or
where we have been and then

we unfurl this map passed down
from one generation to the next,

trace a course traveled, hoped for;
linger in this geography of skin that

tells us no matter where the
journey, we are always here.

Grieving the God of My Youth

I.

I was eleven or so
when He closed up shop,

dismantled the neon sign
that hung outside my bedroom window,
the one that never glowed:
You shall be a BALLERINA. Or,
Become an ASTRONAUT and fly to the moon. Or,
Your destiny is to RIDE HORSES by day
and EAT OREOS—just the creamy insides—by night.

He swung a musty, leather suitcase onto the foot of my bed,
snapped off his flowing, white beard, rolled it up 'til it looked
like a child's furry hand muff and placed it inside.
Large hands then gripped the slender waist of my guardian angel
(who, during this time, had begun to hover less enthusiastically
over my right shoulder),
she went to Him with such force that her halo came askew,
bits of glitter flew from her robe, twinkled to the floor.
He folded her up, taking care to tuck in delicate wings. Then
He pulled a tired-looking broom and dustpan—swept up
shimmery light that crunched like broken stars beneath His feet—
and stuffed it all into the suitcase. All packed up, He snapped
the case closed and slipped out the door.

Light, in the form of headlights
sped across bedroom walls,

swayed below the doorknob
and disappeared.

II. (Dead Jesus)

Around this time, the new priest took down our dead, wooden Jesus and put up another, the risen One. Suspended over the altar by two chains, this Risen Christ with child-like hands on full, outstretched arms, beckoned and was shunned by those who wanted their dead One back.

Too young to know any differently, I leapt and used the flowing metal body as stepping stones. My soul would stretch, take hold of tiny fingers and reach this swinging cross made just for me. Enfolded in Love, we'd sway unseen, above pews drowning in solemn faces. See how the Spirit blows, lifts you up into the hands of Love. Come into this cross made just for you.

Grotesque, mrs. o'reilly whispered into her black glove. *A travesty* her friend agreed. Swinging high above their heads, we sang with joy, our breath stirred the air and still, they felt nothing. We were sad for them, so many wanting their dead Jesus back.

Years went by.

They missed the skin bleached by pain, the crown of tangled thorns that gripped the brow, nails pounded into flesh, the blood, the broken.

Grownups, I concluded, need their Jesus wounded. Dead weight, though, is so much harder to carry. How much they were missing, too afraid to set their dead One free.

III. (Dead Jesus Returns)

I was away at college when the new priest turned old. Take your Christ with you, the people told him. My mother told me this. She had always liked the Risen Christ. *A piece of art, it makes you think*, she'd said. I wondered: if she had been like them, preferred the eyes-closed-can't-hold-you-now-I'm-busy-dying-Jesus, would I have swung? She must have been a stepping stone.

I imagined the old priest carrying out his cross, on his back, the chains dragging behind him, no one to help.

Their Jesus returned and they nailed him up. Once again.

Cruddy Knees

i.
My patellas have been riding high all my life.
Never knew it until the orthopedic surgeon tapped out
a femoral groove, a mix of funk and joint effusion.

Music, degraded to level three, blew out of his shiny pen;
it was hard to hear. *Buy a ranch house. Don't squat or kneel.
Go neither up nor down.* Just to be sure, though, he

danced with my knees. The old gals tried their best
to keep up. They crackled like kindling, shadows
of winces waltzed across his face.

ii.
Dinner party conversations can often be a reach.
My kneecaps are one inch too high, I tell the man
next to me. *One inch?* he gasps.
You told me one centimeter, my friend says.
Same thing, I say. *No it's not,* everyone chimes in.
She's a poet, my friend explains. *Oh,* the man says.
My point is this: any distance throws off the entire dance.

iii.
I tell my physical therapist
patella in Latin means pan
or small dish; may also be a disease olive trees bear.
Doesn't surprise me, she says. *Dish in Spanish is plato.*

I do not tell her I once rented an apartment in Pittsburgh
that shook when the train went by. Come November,
tin pans filled with water rattled on top of radiators,
offerings devoured by the dry mouth of winter.

We are not built to live as long as olive trees, she says.
Only as long as knees can carry us.

iv.
My mother and sister have much in common: shopping, shoe size,
the list goes on. My mother and I have this: cruddy knees.

I have to wear mine another decade or so as I am *too young*;
a new knee lasts only so long before it must be replaced.

Her knees are crooked cousins whispering secrets
as they labor down darkened hallways.

The knee is a hinge, a door she finally agrees
must open.

I want to kneel, whisper *thank you* to my
mother's knees but my own protest

so I bow from hips. *I'll miss you, Knees.*
Can we see you off with a party?

Shut up, shut up, my sister says,
shutters her ears.

Losing parts,
no matter how stormy, terrifies.

v.
Certain cells under stars know their positions.
Starfish grow back arms, hydras their heads,
flatworms rebuild entire bodies. As creatures

who crave to live past expiration dates, we
pull back earth's crust, extract titanium, and
fashion fake parts.

My doctor-of-infectious-disease brother is in
the business of missing parts. Before he cleaves
an arm from his patient, she fancies herself

a starfish. *A new one grows back, right?* she smiles.
We are big animals, he tells her. *Only tips of fingers
and toes come back to us if we're lucky.*

vi.
In mature olive groves, pruning is best done in autumn,
after fruit has been harvested.

The Trouble with Reading In Your Hometown

She is there, in the second row, as you enter the third to last stanza, the mother of the boy you kissed in 10th grade at some party. He pressed hard, like a piranha. When you pulled away, bits of your flesh clung to his metal smile. You can't remember his name because it was his older brother you had the crush on. That was before his father was dead, his mother stepped out of the closet and you swam away to be schooled by more fish.

The audience applauds.

Like the Parents They Never Knew

Between goldenrod and phlox, her world gently sails—
canvas of white silk, trail of loose letters,
love path of m's or z's ensnares his heart.
So, the next flower over, he builds a humble home.

Soon he'll call on her,
make his way to the edge of the masterpiece
she dismantles, consumes and redesigns
each day.

The moment his feet touch her silk,
he shudders and shudders, feels her weight.
Three times his size, she is golden, her abdomen
could hold a thousand eggs. He shudders.

He comes to know her by brushing his legs—
the first and second pair—against hers, rubs them
along her abdomen, then draws his legs to mouth,
tastes her scent. Finding her pleasing, he continues
to court by cutting out a section of elaborate lines.
Intrigued, she permits these edits.

He casts out one simple line
then hangs upside down, his feet
plucking string of shimmering harp.
He dances up and down, wags his abdomen to and fro—
wafting her world. She cannot hold back
and scurries to him.

There, on the mating thread, all those legs
and legs and legs conspire. His heart slows.
He dies, sealing hope inside her.

II: The Holy Family

Castaways

Here, we have all the bamboo we'll ever need.
Everyone eats. The millionaires and the least
of us sleep in huts. Everyone, except maybe
the Professor, wastes time planning to escape
paradise.

Even those of us brave and sure as the Skipper
get caught up in the storm of life with little buddies
who, no matter how hard or little they work, bungle
our best schemes.

We dwell in private lagoons, distracted,
at times, by fortune or women in gold lame
who swish by and wink away their power.
Travelers stranded on this good Earth,
we rise up only so far before we fall.

Before Russell Johnson landed
the Professor gig on Gilligan's Island
and tinkered with coconut shells
and seawater to charge radio batteries,

his B-24 was shot down
during World War II. He landed
on the Philippine island of Mindanao.
Hard sand broke both ankles.

Maestro

                Hair a jangle of frayed notes,
he is a composition of loss, knows the gritty
rhythm of this unhushed world. Found his
one bright A years ago in the back alley of
Shale's Pub. Won't let it go. Picks up the
abandoned keys of B and C. Stick in hand,
he points to the darkened sky.

                  In the downbeat,
wind thrums litter and leaves; rain strikes
hi-hats of canned refuse. A brief reprieve,
the whispered din of diners, then a chorus
of cars gears up, lights and horns blazing.
Arms sweep wildly now, his stick a blur.
With a nod, he cues the soloist who's just
flown in. Donning a pale blue dress, bodice
dripping in green and purple, tenderly she
croons. This stirs hearts in the balcony of
branches, dapper fellows, each dressed in
brown suits, they sway as one.

                      He bows low,
takes and tucks what sings to him—
a single shoe—under his wing, dragging
two black bags—tux tails—behind him.

Psoriasis Siren

Her mother and her mother's mother had it.
Just like her, from the torso on down.
No real cure, the cause a mystery.

It skipped her seven siblings,
the eldest sister growing only a small patch,
easily concealed by garments.

While it takes a month to shed their skins—
produce smooth coats of fresh cells,
polished pink—

she changes hers every three to four days,
yet the dead skin hangs on,
refuses to slough off.

It hugs her hips, builds up 'round her buttocks,
drapes thighs. Spangled in silver scales,
she hides her shine,

slinking away to rocks by the sea,
their coolness eases her discomfort—
a trick she learned from her mother.

When, at the tender age of ten
sleep becomes difficult,
she takes to the tub for naps

then enters the teenage years

elegizing her days, drags herself around,
skin over skin, tombstone after toppled tombstone.

At twenty, her mother dies.
She slips underwater.
Rumors swirl.

Eventually, she will come up for air,
hoping to be a meadow,
free of stones.

Optimal Foraging Theory

With progeny scattered across the country,
kinfolk have grown ravenous, must
forage far for sustenance. To augment
energy, they travel in packs, supporting

the supposition applied to bands of both
roving animals and in-laws, an equation
that looks like this: $$\frac{E}{h+s}$$

The big E is energy stolen from another.

Despite its diminutive size,
h houses the handling of time—
the time it takes to draw near, devour, and digest,
the time it takes the clan to shuffle into the Dodge Caravan,

drive across the state, park, walk up the winding path,
ring the bell, ignore surprised looks on faces of loved ones,
hand over the remaining, dangerously warm deviled eggs, shed suitcases,

and trample over weekend plans.

To conserve E, the clan lift nary a finger,
except to gorge on grandchildren and hasty casseroles.
Stuffed full, the h takes on the s of searching
for the next meal.

On Sunday, as the Caravan backs out of the driveway,

the herd swings into full *s* mode. Slinging dates out windows,
they synch their calendars into the horizon, keen for the next bite.

The rate of *E* astonishes.

The Great Shrinking Scare of 1985

This is a true story except that, when referring to the male member, the term star will be used, as in star light, star bright, first star I see tonight.

It is midnight in China, when an eighteen-year-old awakens to discover his star shrinking. He shrieks. Families and neighbors rush to his side and before it disappears completely, they catch the fading light in their hands and thump him with branches from a peach tree. They beat drums and set off firecrackers. *We'll catch the ghost*, they tell him, confident in the power of the peach, knowing it's a reliable host for trapping evil spirits. They repeat the process until the star fully returns to its owner.

Others are not so lucky. Walking down the street, men's stars abandon them at the slightest brush of another man's robes. *Thief!* they shout. While police prefer not to handle a case of a missing star, some inspect the scene of the crime. Much to the men's surprise, they see their star returned, twinkling against a curl of cloud. Some men insist it's just a flicker of what once was, an understudy, a starlet standing in for the real one.

The Succulent Ones

i. The Plant

Beneath fleshy leaves of aloe,
roots hover near the surface,
nibble on sweet nothings.

ii. The Botanist

She cleaves to memories,
soaks up the juicy past,
calls upon reserves.

iii. The Boyfriend

In this parched place in which
only the succulent survive, he
snaps her arm in half and drags
her tonic across his arid heart.

The Word Whoreder

She tells the psychiatrist she isn't sure how
it got this way, that maybe it was her
father's fault that she played with

plebeians then shoved them under sofa cushions,
slipped somnolent and sully under the mattress
stashed miserly and magnitude in the sugar jar.

It began slowly, content just to
spend quiet evenings at home with laconic
and laissez-faire. But then her father died,

and within days she brought home
obstreperous, loquacious, and
alacrity—partied with them for weeks

before she realized loquacious
had pushed laconic and laissez-faire
out the door. Inchoation slips out

from under her tongue—she acknowledges
it's gotten out of hand. *It's not easy living
like this*, she says standing before stacks

of hubris towering in front of the fireplace;
she can't even brush her teeth without stumbling
over garrulous piles of you-name-it.

She weaves her way
like a drunken mouse
gnawing through a

cache of wanton words—
dingy, salacious, crapulence—
all hailing down upon her,

admits she can't stop,
tastes shrink in her mouth,
purrs, *I want even you.*

As Saturn Turns

She wears her womb
on the outside,
hula of ice and cold.

You'd think she'd tire
after 4 ½ billion years but
there she goes, giving birth
again.

On the edge of her A ring
a baby moon—a mere half mile—
peeks its milky head into the

churning brood of 62 siblings,
each busy blazing a trail
around their cold and distant mother.

Each appears unable to gain
their mother's affections—
save for Encelaus
whose watery eruptions
cause Saturn to slow
her rotation ever
so slightly.

Yet Saturn's children press on.
Mima with her ravaged face,
big sister Rhea and her icy stare.
Titan, the golden boy, too dense

to offer up salacious details
of the family's turbulent past.

Phoebe gave up vying for
love billions of years ago,
struck a path opposite the others.
Hyperion's spongy face just absorbs
whatever is or isn't hurled his way.

The twins, Prometheus and Pandora,
are too busy herding their mamma's rings
to notice the drama swirling around them.

Meanwhile…
800 million miles away
on planet Earth,

a father-to-be
mouses over the blip
of baby moon scientists
have already named Peggy.

She is clearer than the grainy
picture of his own 2 ½ inch
(crown to rump)

nameless walnut that hangs
on the refrigerator door,
orbited by two brightly

colored magnets
the size of dimes.

Sending the Dogs Off

for Kris

We have scattered them now
these thin but muscular beasts
that hungered for scraps
of kindness.

Broken and beaten,
we washed and washed
their wariness down,
whispered in shredded ears.

Their language purloined,
some listened with ears
cropped, tails docked,

sinewy strands
of fragile boldness
knitting together
beneath our fingertips.

There is no
forcing
hope,

but it sputters
here and there
as when,

the tail—
intending to swish—
shudders.

Small Prayer for Margaret

She rolls over, lumbers
into the thin skin of sleep;
down she rumbles.

Her breath slows, blows
steady through old white pines,
that once held up the sky.

    *

Trees of Peace,
Iroquois called them.
Dream now of lifting pine.

Bury the hatchet, the arrows,
and feelings of war,
then stretch the earth

back over bared roots,
sealing peace under
a blanket of earth.

    *

She tugs the covers.
Like a mother
I watch her breathe,

worry that when she

awakens, she will shed
this skin of old world,

thunder against the new,
discover—again—the tree
she leaned against, felled.

    *

Natives harvested
pine sap to heal
wounds of all kinds,

chewed needles
in winter
to stay alive.

    *

Uprooted from slumber,
she pierces through
the hard bark

of wakefulness,
emerges roaring
and kicking her feet.

    *

Resin of hope
hold fast
to a timbered life.

They played Brady Bunch on Saturdays

Being the youngest, she was relegated
to small parts. (Alice, Cousin Oliver,
Sam, but mostly Alice.)

Go bake us some cookies, Bobby would say.
Yeah, chimed in Greg and Marsha.
While you are at it, make our beds, Jan
and Peter were fond of saying.
Mike would often demand: *Tell Sam
to bring us some meat.*

Fuck you, she'd think as she threw
blankets over dirty sheets, picked up
a shoe and ordered tender cuts of beef,
or crumpled washcloths into mounds
and served them to the whole damn
bunch on a wilted spatula. Carol
would chuckle and say, *Oh, Alice.*

She missed the dead wife, the one
they never spoke of, who came
before Carol with her shag.
One day, she decided she'd
had enough and quit.
You can't quit, they all moaned.
Who will pack our lunches now?

Searching

Her nose drips
green pepper,
small mounds of moist
meat round out chin and cheeks.
Mary on meatloaf.

Her son is turning up in odd locations—
on a clean, crumpled sock in England.
In the States, he's seared himself into a stick of fish,
burnt his profile into a wedge of Texas toast.
Somewhere else, her snack-sized son is a Cheeto
curled in prayer.

She wants to lean on Joseph, tell him
this is no way to save the world
but her husband is nowhere to be found.
So Mary gathers up her congealed veil of holy
and seeps into the whorled, wooden door
of the Riddle family trailer.

She is closing in on her boy,
every grain of her being ablaze.

Subpoenaing the Dead

If Scott Panetti got his way
Jesus Christ and Anne Bancroft
would have come to his defense.
Like some kind of miracle workers
they could have explained to the jury
how, for years he'd worked hard to stop
the devil—tried washing him off walls
'til hands bled, buried his parent's
Satan-saturated couch and fiendish lamps
in the backyard, nailed shut the curtains
to keep from being captured on film.

But Scott never gets his way.
They've always been out to get him.
So he saddles up, fires his lawyers,
and dressed in a purple cowboy costume
explains why Sarge made him kill
his ex-wife's parents.

His ramblings spur him on to death row
where he preaches the Gospel to inmates.
He doesn't want to die; he wants to giddy-up
for God. But, if the Lone Star State gets its way,
they're gonna look him in the eye and shoot him up
with pentobarbital.

Satan, all the while, sedately waits.

Having Bought St. Joseph, I Bury Him

Hundreds of years ago, when nuns needed more land to build convents, they buried St. Joseph medals and prayed to this patron saint of family and household needs. Today, thousands of home sellers and real estate agents have adopted this practice, burying a statuette upside down on the property of the home. The St. Joseph Statue, "Your Underground Real Estate Agent Kit" has "everything thing you need to successfully bury your own St. Joseph Statue. Be it fact or be it fiction, it's worked more than once."

St.JosephStatue.com

My unchurched friend
tells me it is well past time,
so, unaided, as rain

mixed with pine and
thick as molasses seeps
into my bent back,

I pry open the earth
with a trowel, dig a
simple grave—

a watchful place
from which he will
mind the white house

with black shutters.
I press his plastic body
cloaked in a peach robe

headfirst,

into the swollen
ground;

place a pinecone
atop his
hollow feet,

then run to the car
my body drawing
back drapes

of rain.
In my haste
I will forget

the most
important part
of the burial instructions:
You must pray to him,
this earthly father,
to intercede on your behalf.

Later, I will tell
my friend that because
I was infused in faith—

which wasn't orderly
at all but soiled
and sticky with resin—

I don't bother
to clean my hands, just
let them speak

for themselves,
seize the wheel
and drive away.

Sriracha: Sultan of Sauce

Praise be your makers at Huy Fong Food Factory.
Sun ripened jalapeños harvested, then blended with
just the right amounts of vinegar, garlic, salt, and sugar.

You slip slowly through rooster-tattooed body,
red washing through wattle, cock, and comb.
You are my daily prayer.

Oh king of condiments, citizens of Irwindale
suffer your sting and sue, raising the hackles of
addicts who want them to take the heat for the team.

Remember this: the eater brings their own heat to the meal.

Be strong Huy Fong. Do not fear. The faithful fight this battle
on the vast landscape of the world wide web. They march
into unknown blogs, pepper the unedited terrain of comment sections.

One Sriracha soldier, going by "Mitt Romney" takes a stand.
I know I'm going to hell for this, but I put the sauce on everything I eat.
"Ann Romney" backs him up. *It's true. He even puts it on me.*

Ambushes are frequent. "Neighbor Next Door" cries out, *We
were here first!*
Out of nowhere, "Derk" fires off, *If they think the sauce smells bad
they should smell my sweaty ball sack.*

Remember this: the eater brings their own heat to the meal.

"Hoarding in Texas," goes awol, uses his last paycheck
to wipe out his local Foodarama, lest a judge rule Huy Fong
cease and desist. "Pacifist Pete," hunkers down, hoping
the government will create an Affordable Condiment Act.

Remember. The eater brings their own heat to the meal.

"Barry" is suffering flashbacks, reliving his tour on Avery Island
where he and his first grade classmates vomited their field trip
away outside the tangy Tabasco factory. "Bad mom" confesses
to putting it in her kid's baby formula. "Lander" doesn't give a shit.

But what can be more important
than this moment when, after dawn breaks,
a cock may soon crow somewhere?

Back when hair bows were in fashion

Susan Smith thought she'd wrapped up the case in '94 when she
    told the town her lost
sons were kidnapped by a black man. She touched the white bow
    at the back of her hair,
adjusted it just so for the cameras. Nine days after looking for a man
    that never was, she
admitted to strapping her boys into their car seats, releasing the hand
    break, and watching
the Mazda Protégé roll down the boat ramp and into John D. Long Lake.

Ever since, mothers have been driving children into ponds at alarming
    rates.

In Texas a drunk mother drove her two children into a pond on
    Halloween. In Tennessee,
a five-year old called 911 Thanksgiving morning from the car her drunk
    mom plunged
into a pond. In Minnesota, a young mother steered into an icy pond. She
    swam to shore
and wailed as two of the five children drowned.

What is it about ponds that draw these mothers near—womb-like tombs,
    rushing nowhere?

In this isolated depression, a mother seeks respite from the mire.
She casts out worries, gives into the murk that cocoons her brood—learns
    too late
that with hope tethered to the bottom lip of a pond, release never comes.

Sketch of life form at library

I'm able as shit his arm says.
Shrieks it, actually, in all caps,
like this: I'M ABLE
                AS SHIT

No period and not one librarian
to shush him. No boss to take
him up on this offer that bleeds

greenish grey from his mouthless
arm. Hand with four fingers
and a lightning bolt of thumb

clutch a paperback—
Pebble in the Sky
by Isaac Asimov.

As his eyes suck up words
about tomorrow, oily rivers
of hair stream past his nose

which drips three silver rings.
Everything in his orbit
is in a constant state of falling.

Where are you, Lilly? whispers
an interloper, dangerously close.
It's time to go. Lilly? Distance

is nothing. The universe, collapsing,
I'M-ABLE-AS-SHIT rises and places
what world he has left on his back.

The House that Jack Built

An old woman walks into a shoe
the one that Jack built by candlelight

with nimble hands. He wasn't always
agile. Once, as a child,

he'd gone up a jagged terrain with a boy
he found fetching. It didn't go well.

The boys fell and Jack mangled his foot.
Late at night the pail,

sloshing with memories of Gil, tumbles still,
empties its tinny voice inside his crown.

He stuffs the watery down, marries a woman,
nice and soft who doesn't seem to mind his limp.

He builds a shoe big enough to hold them both
but she outgrows the place, her plumpness

puffing out of windowed eyelets,
sealing out the chance for sun; she oozes away.

Jack stays, laces fingers over his hungry belly
and leans against the worn tongue.

With everything curved, there is no danger
of snagging loose a memory. In time,

he steps out at night, into the leathery air,
to build his shoe the partner it didn't have.

Years pass. He peers through a hole in the heel.
It's just the old woman across the way,

her children grown and gone,
her house pleasingly bare save for beans

draining in a colander upon the shank.
A husky thought unfurls, a stalk, streaking through

his mind; he's hobbled through this world a bruise,
telling himself he needed shoes to climb.

Cotton Candy Lady, Corner of Fifth & Wood

Hair an airy beehive of spun sugar, she chomps on gossip, flosses gums with fairies, tosses them aside. Rim of leaves and small twigs honey the hem of hot pink pants. Fingers buzz up from a swarm of toffee-colored briefcases to pluck threads of shiny conversations. Take care what you say. Everything sticks. Wind stings her face, blue eyes cloud; lost in a swirling confection of ties that rise like tongues.

World's Greatest Extra

He's a hand no one holds.
A mouth no one hears.

It's coming up on ten years
he's been blending in,

a hidden extra no one
whines about,

living life unnoticed.
He's just a face in the crowd,

except for that time, with legs dangling
off the back of a truck, he played clarinet.

Right now he's a back hunched
over a bar, drinking in the notion

they don't want all of him
even though his parts are all here.

He waits for his cue to disappear.
As rain pools into a puddle of dark

he leaves, but not before his shoe enters,
takes center stage.

She Stops Seeing Her Beauty at Age Seven

She recalls the first time she died.
It was thirty years ago while wearing a yellow dress.

"My lovely lemon girl!" mamma said that morning
as she weaved tender-headed hair into two thick braids.

Lemon girl sat straight and pretty, hands folded on desk,
felt a tap on her left shoulder and turned around.

Blonde girl waited for the smile, then: *Nappy head!*
Nappy head! The class joined in, clipping budding wings.

The teacher's voice sheared through the chanting:
What do you want to be called?

Colored? she whispered. The teacher smiled,
feel of mamma's fingers took flight; lemon girl gone.

Over the years, the deaths kept coming, here, a little there,
sprinkled like fine sugar over caramel skin and days like

just this morning when she ached to turn around
but could not bear one more death.

She died at home, moments after slipping
a blue dress over her head.

As coffee grew cold, it took everything
to stand there, as if nothing was wrong,

as a blue hydrangea in a lime vase
gave pause between her and a young girl at play.

Zombie Mommy

He has been watching her disappear
for weeks now.

A fading bruise, she staggers
into the kitchen mumbling something,

then pours Life into a bowl
for the last time.

He thinks of how his father
used to praise her cooking.

Tearing meat from the bone
with his greasy teeth, he'd say,

how tender you make everything, hon
and she would smile a small smile.

He is too young to know that
these memories are decaying inside her,

shredding apart even her finest thought:
that she is his mother.

She spills the milk,
doesn't bother to clean it up.

He notices the left tip of her nose is gone,
has splashed into the tiny world sloshing below

his chin. He pushes away her offering.
As the fin of a grey shark circles the last grains of hope

he drowns in one inch of thought—
that even though past the point of healing
                                          he loves her still.

To all the B saints

You pay attention to the barbers and bankers, look out for the boy scouts—ready or not here they come to merit the day and oh, yes, let us not forget the builders, the bi-racial, the betrothed.

To you B saints looking out for the blind and the broken, and to all those bending in times of trouble for bowels and breasts, directly beseeching on behalf of brides and even that bachelor wearing a boutonniere of bruises.

A toast to the brewers, a pat to the bakers, flicking Bics to the candlestick makers falling in with the C saints, the alphabet of holy marching on.

Lists

i.

We were a list-making people, anthropologists of the future will conclude, uncovering evidence of lives stitched together by lists. They will follow long trails of mostly loose, sloppy stitches; unearth in other places thready lives lived small and tight. In a few locations they will learn that hems of hearts hung ragged, stitches ripped out. They will place their fingers over tell-tale holes made by the prick of a pin, never quite healed over.

ii.

I once kept a secret list of all the things I had lost.

iii.

Living by lists can drive a person to madness. I once had a neighbor who asked me to care for her cat while she was away. I followed her four-page list of typed instructions and still, the cat died. She never spoke to me again, but she wrote a note that looked like this:

> *I do not*
> *blame you*
> *for the demise*
> *of Eubie.*
> *Feline Leukemia*
> *played a role.*

iv.

Some lists I feel guilty for jotting down so I crumple them up and throw them away. Lists like the one entitled: *stuff my mother-in-law gave me*. Several pages long, it cited items such as:

1. homemade applesauce,
2. underwear she eventually wanted back,
3. ceramic pumpkin napkin ring holders,
4. two packages of googly eyes,
5. a slew of articles clipped neatly from magazines, usually *How to...*
   be a better parent, keep your husband happy, cook goulash five ways, make eggshell crafts on snowy days, turn scraps of felt into giant animals, recycle your old bras. Articles like that.

I try not to read too much into them, just tell myself my mother-in-law enjoys cutting rectangular shapes out of paper and giving them to me any chance she can. She also litters my life with

her son's past—
      a. school papers and art projects throughout his elementary career. Like I care that he scored 96% on his third grade
           math test,
      b. an ashtray made in shop class that resembles a heap of dung,
      c. one marching band hat, the bane of my existence
         once fluffy white, now clotted grey
            like somebody sucked on it here and there,
         left it to dry and stiffen,
      d. a faded t-shirt with a Xeroxed face of a girl, a gift from his high school
    girlfriend, Jan.

v.

Because I'm not his mother I've throw everything out with the exception of the applesauce which our son ate and the band hat which my husband refuses to part with because *you never know when something like this might come in handy.*

And, for some inexplicable reason, I kept the t-shirt with Jan on it, relegated it to my sock drawer. Twice already I've pulled it out, put it on, stood before the mirror and noticed how my breasts filled out Jan's rosy cheeks, contorted her lip-glossed pout into an uncomfortable grimace.

vi.

I'll engrave lists in my mind. Take for example, Jan, the one-dimensional girlfriend, confined by a sea of white. Note that feathered bangs frame a pale face, tilted just so. Her chin rests upon clasped hands from which bare arms slide down into elbows sunk in darkness. Pilled cotton, like fuzzy pimples threatens to engulf once flawless skin.

vii.

Lists, like drowsy dresses, strung together on lines, pinched by wooden fingers, that no matter how hard they hold on—flutter then fade.

III. In the Meantime

Waiting and Entering

Scattered throughout the country are keys
waiting for hands that have hidden them.

Quietly, without complaint,
they pass the time—
resting inside faux rocks,
lounging on ledges and under dusty mats,
hanging from hooks and rusty nails,
sitting under the infamous chipped flowerpots
of this world.

When their time finally comes
thin, grooved bodies
must be pressed into remembering;
they have to be jiggled, turned, cajoled,
and convinced to crack open
this moment for which they were made.

Remember When Corn Was Corn

Passing through Kinde where armies
of corn stand at attention

my father who is driving says, *Did you know that some
of your genetic material started just south of Flint?*

This unhinges a memory—a man I met at a party.
Nothing good comes from corn, he'd said.

He would know. He farms land passed down
from his daddy whose daddy handed it on down to him.

Grew all kinds of crops then. Just grow corn now.
As if to apologize: *That's how the boss wants it.*

I didn't realize farmers had bosses. Must have said this aloud
as he added, *Yeah, Monsanto's boss in these here parts.*

My father's voice breaks in: *We are just
five hours from where your relatives farmed.*

Is corn there still corn, growing unencumbered?
Or is it like the corn here, precisely numbered rows

of 37Y12, 37Y12, pressing in on the right
and 37Y12, 37Y12, 37Y12 on the left

Troops of 37Y14's swell under the command
of Pioneer, rising hard out of this brave new world,

yielding. My father drives cautiously
through this minefield of sameness,

a flash of Integra Experimental 38A57 up ahead,
near Dave's Auto, an explosion of 97Y30.

Eventually we leave numbers behind, think
we've slipped through the town unharmed.

Autotomy, Self-Amputation

Under threat and in the grip of another,
some bodies, born with built-in lines of weakness, let go,
lose a bit of self—a tail, a leg, a memory—
scuttle away to live one more day.

What's gone weighs heavy, those great claws left behind
on beaches and jungles of boardrooms where we've diminished
ourselves, resumed with stumps instead of stings. Absence,
the damselfly will tell you, devours its own energy.

Under the hard spell of fists against ribs, a woman detaches
and drifts away, hears the beating as a runaway heart,
a mad drummer drumming *I love you. I love you.*

She Was His Favorite Chapter

She acknowledged her body, thanked it
for its years of service, for giving her

hands to plant an oak, arms to
tend to this world, to him,

said goodbye to legs that carried her
line by beautiful line.

She sighed as he ran fingers
down her spine one last time

and then Death
turned the page.

Even still,
he could not put her down,

kept returning to the garden
she left behind.

The voice she no longer had
perfumed the spring,

murmured through mums in fall,
dog-eared his heart

until one particularly blustery day
she fluttered away

landing near the tree
that praised the sky

with outstretched arms,
doing what he could not.

I Want a Church

I want to find me a church
where artisans of peace and justice
tired from practicing their craft
find themselves in pews which
break like waves against the altar,

waves that swell and stretch
anchors of all shapes and sizes,
washing those who have
gathered into this singing place
out again, far and wide
into unknown, dangerous waters.

I want a church
made of sailors who know
that it is not about the boat,
who resist the temptation
to stay on board
and play it safe
for fear of drowning,
or worse yet, that nets cast
will come up empty
and I, you, we will have nothing
to show for our efforts.

I want a church
that celebrates sailors
who step out of the boat

and with wobbly sea legs
stagger onto dry land

and find themselves
just brave enough to
chisel watery souls with love.

Winter Kudzu of Kalamazoo

How
is it,
in less
than 24 hours,

your chin
churns out stubble,
bloats into a bearded boulder

that thunders down the salty streets
beneath me? How is it—after kicking your lowdown puss—

I feel such satisfaction in watching your hoary shrub
break off in one thick chunk,

feel no remorse
as I back over
your disguise
and drive
away?

On Good Friday, Walmart Wants to Save You

You can buy Easter
at the drop of a bonnet.
Sweet savings await

inside a slim insert
printed just for you.
Come, fill yourself,

with creamy Velveeta,
Lean Cuisines, and life
saving jellybeans.

Praise ever creeping colors
of peeps that sour the tongue
of the young, their dotted

eyes lined up in a cheep,
cheep chorus: Eat us!
We are only a dollar, nine.

Here, two eggs, ounces
of goodness on either side
of a Dove transformed—

a baby bunny
that flows with milk
and chocolate,

its pricked, unhearing
ears foiled in gold;
this is the body

you may break.
More Easter
for your money

if only you
hop on over here
and shop, shop, shop.

Look no further
to fill your basket.
Live better with us

and Rachel Ray
cookware, but hurry,
the Star is Bursting.

WHAT WE DO WITH OUR STUFF

Nearly 1 in 10 US households rent a self storage unit; that has increased from 1 in 17 in 1995 – or an increase of approximately 65 percent in the last 15 years.

-Self Storage Association Fact Sheet

Sell it,
Buy it,
Wrap it,
Hang it,
Hide it,
Flaunt it,
Stuff it,
Clean it,
Wear it,
Store it,
Sort it,
Move it,
Insure it,
Break it,
Lose it,
Find it,
Fold it,
Touch it.
Don't touch it.
Slap hands that touch it.
Worry when we don't have it.
Worry when we have it.
Wonder where it all came from
and why we gather it to us?
Wonder, what else, in place of stuff

could something else reside?

How to Become a Virgin

                Realize, regardless
of sex, you have a womb. This
is a place. Any place, where something
of great importance can be conceived. You
must seek it out and then line the womb in trust.
Many deem this difficult and give up. As bolts of
trust are often impossible to find, we suggest patching
scraps together. Toss out the notion that it must shimmer
like satin. Fur, faux or otherwise is not advised. Some will
find wool favorable, a scratchy reminder which irritates until
say, a pearl is formed. For others, leaves or delicate wings of
insects work best. You will feel tired and, at times, worry that
you are not up to the task. Be patient. This is the trickiest part.
Anywhere from one week to years later, you will feel a tug, a
kicking of heels within. Place both hands on belly of a tree.
Feel it leap inside you. You will be overcome.
You will not be lucky.

Protecting the Boys

Dunham's Sports is a desert depleted of helpful clerks.

Mother and son stand before rows of cups that hang from pegs
and swagger with names like "The Boss," "The Trophy,"
and "The Hammer."

She plucks a cup—tiny as a petal—that should be named
"Small Shield," less of a cup, more like a bike helmet a mouse
might strap on should it need to zoom, zoom away from a cat
on the prowl.

She holds it over his boy parts, perhaps in the wrong direction.
When you get older, she tells the son on the cusp of nine, *don't
always listen to "The Boss."*
What? he asks. *Nothing,* she replies.

He settles on a Louisville Slugger, boy's extra large. "Bionic Cup"
the package touts.

Home and two hours before practice she'll find him sprawled
on the couch, in full uniform, cup already cradling his crotch.
He'll look up from the bowl of goldfish crackers resting
on his belly.

From the smile on his face,
she knows her boy is already sliding into home plate.
                         He wants to be ready for the world.

If You Could Stand on Saturn

A speck of light we are
a smudge of brilliance
amidst ever expanding darkness

not yet even a blue marble.

Zoom in eight hundred million miles.
Land on the flat but sloping roof
of Paris Cleaners in Kalamazoo.

The premiere destination for dirty clothes since 1903!

Look up while standing on this one story,
purple painted tower of Pisa
swathed in neon signage.

See, at times, Saturn with your naked eyes.
Take hold of binoculars, behold the gas giant's swirling rings
as beneath your feet

generations of launderers
clean sundry spots from shirts, faces blazing
as they press crisp pleats, pant after pant, steam rising.

Return to Saturn.

You will not know when
one by one glass tube letters
burn out, the S in Paris destroyed

by a small stone thrown from the hand
of a boy. You will see none of this,
nor know that forming glass letters,

and injecting into neon gas
a precise mix of metal and dust
to create a wash of colors

is a dying art.

Magnetic Findings in the Czech Republic

> "Several mammalian species spontaneously align their body axis with respect to the Earth's magnetic field (MF) lines in diverse behavioral contexts… With this in mind we searched for signs of magnet alignment in dogs…"
> Hart et al. "Dogs are Sensitive to Small Variations of the Earth's Magnetic Field," Frontiers in Zoology, 2013.

Scientists licked by the salty shores
of the North, Baltic, and Black Sea
discover that dogs tune in to
the dance of Earth.

Like cattle, red and roe deer,
dogs find it pleasing to align
their furry bodies with the spine
of this planet.

They romp through magnetic fields,
pausing only to pee
along the North-South axis
of their grand and ever spinning world

shared with those who call themselves Master,
and navigate by a thousand metal suns
they've tossed into the sky, who
calibrate their doings by clicks

and cluck *what a shame they've lost their way*
when birds sink from the skies and whales
barrel out of oceans onto sandy shores.
Dogs refuse to leave best friends, stick

close by, drag tongues over even the most
dull-eyed in the pack, the unseasonably astray,
and those who live so loud they will never
hear themselves home.

What We Don't Tell Our School Volunteers

You have been assigned to a tropical storm.
She is forming in a relatively warm school,
the outer edge of her frayed, but eyes calm, still.
You are in the socket of the storm; don't be fooled.

Strong winds gather in her bones, energy derived
from the evaporation of soft things—a mother,
a good night's sleep. Losses recondense, form
waves that wear down whatever fine thing is left.

Her father, having endured sustained winds for years,
is swept away by part-time jobs that blow in clothes
or food but not both and that is why the girl winces as she
shambles from class to you in shoes two sizes too small.

When you open the workbook and say, *Alicia, your
teacher suggests we begin on page seven*, she will
taste the sound of her name, full and lush as a pear,
hold onto, for days, what has been plucked just for her.

Week after week, you'll sit in a tiny chair, battered
in a bumpy stream of sentences as Alicia
drags her chewed-up fingernail along a path lit
by a shard of moon that hangs from a ragged sky.

As pressure builds, fight the urge to sweep
this gathering storm of girl into your pocket
and head for home. You must not mistake

the beating heart for yours.

There will come a time you wish
you had never signed on. It will pass.
Despite the bleak forecast, do not give up.
Know that warm air, lighter than cold, must rise.

Imagine Alicia breezing into the harbor,
see her moor herself to a mountain, tango
with the clouds, come momentarily
to rest near the slip with her name on it.

Until then, hang on,
keep reading and feeding her pears.

Upon Reading the Settlement Agreement in Re: to Lyondell Chemical Company, *et al.*,

I apologize for the unwieldy,
rather ugly title of this poem
but could find no way to liquidate.

Whereas;
'Lo the memo lost
confirming that children
in Michigan, Maryland, Pennsylvania, Oklahoma, Idaho, Iowa, New Jersey,
Illinois, North Carolina, Georgia, Texas and California,
are doing what children do…

With respect to (i) climbing beanstalks,
(ii) drinking water, (iii) breathing air,
notwithstanding water and air
simmering in pots, stirred by a Giant.

Whereas;
The Giant complains
his chemical arm has grown tired,
seeks relief from cleaning up
the mess he has made.

Now, therefore
might just get away,
be told that it is okay, that this
clotted, clouded kitchen shall be
considered neat and tidy

all in order, as long as
one half of a dish
to every 100 dishes
—one half of one—is clean.

Whereas,
this talk of covenants
a matter settled,
with stroke of pen
instead of shovel.

Whereas,
the United States is
on behalf of the EPA,
Department of Interior,
Federal Trustees

where is, in this
lowest priority of claims,
the Department of Justice
on behalf of children?

Pursuant to
above matters,
where
are you?

Doctrine on the Primacy and Infallibility of Digital Billboards and Such

I.

Call it
a religion, a trinity:
advertiser, agency, consumer;

an unspoken creed upheld
that if two lights are good,
then thousands are better.

It takes energy to praise this way.
We, the faithful,
lit day and night,

consumed by the glow of it all
baptize our children—drenching them
in the true light of digital billboards

sacrificing trees to the God of Progress,
a growing congregation—tv on a stick—
cropping up alongside roads and highways.

Each shiny new follower shouting out
one hundred tons of CO_2 a year,
a catechism of carbon dioxide dogmas.

Together, we are building
a well-littered path of faith.

Praise be to Progress!

It will take us somewhere.

II.

The world, though,
feeling the weight
of this fervent flock,

is finding it harder
and harder to uphold
the inerrancy of thy ways.

III.

Fireflies—
earth's home
made stars—

pulsed wildly
in the era
of Eden.

These tiny
prophetic impulses
must be pushed aside,

thy radiant hosts
swallowed
whole.

This is
no time
to ache

for the ancient
light
of lesser gods.

Obsession #248: Moths

Here, the night sky hums.
In Borneo, Hawkmoths
jiggle their parts

above heads
of lovers
unaware

as they incline
toward each other
a crescendo of

high-pitched notes
will tumble from
the sky,

jamming
a hungry bat's
sonar detector,

rendering
even the smallest
of sighs

invisible.

Dandelions

This day, drenched in sun and green
a hundred and more dandelions sparkle
yet, I'm only seeing them now, having
shrugged off their wonders years ago.

The Tuscarora, whose arms were once
wide enough to hug the Great Lakes,
noticed these tiny miracles blooming
when the sturgeon began to run.

Sturgeon, swimming back from near
extinction, considered a nuisance, too,
their large and bony bodies tearing
the white man's fishing nets.

What happens to us when we leave
miracles on shores to rot or feed to pigs?
When we mow miracles down by millions
and spray them blind, like I want to do

right now to the dandelions gone to seed,
soft heads bobbing on slender stalks,
leafy arms, jagged like lion's teeth
chomping into this lawny life?

Ancient wonders, riding chariots of wind,
when did my neighbors and I stop caring
for you? Listen, eggs are hatching.
As sturgeon larvae drift downstream

let us be dandelion warriors again. We'll smear
our faces; streaked in the color of old bones,
we'll run through the streets, greeting our loves
with bouquets of a dozen suns.

Later, standing still and blowing moon heads,
we'll join in the miracles, sailing stars across
the neighborhood that, no matter what, return
each year to greet us with glowing.

Longing for the Dynamite Days

It was a time when one had the luxury of nursing
a fondness for TNT, could

give in to one's penchant for throwing
pies in the face
or, on days when a little more felt in order, build
a Burmese tiger trap

ordered from ACME,
a good old American Company
that Made Everything.

Ah, to know your nemesis
like Tweetie knew Putty Cat,
Jerry knew Tom and that never-veering-from-the-road
Road Runner knew Wile E. Coyote.

You could always count on them being up to
something looney somewhere.

   It was a time when gravity
      was the greatest thing to fear
a plank of wood wedged under a boulder
   teetering high on the cliff above one's head.

Characters folded flat, slim as dollar bills
you tucked into the warmth of your wallet,
crumpled like muslin, turning up
with nary a scratch in the next exchange.

The worst to be suffered was humiliation
in this simpler time of cactus and road
dog houses, aprons and chicken coops.

Everyone never quite succeeding
but never giving up.

As re-runs play over and over
mailboxes, you worry, are becoming a thing of the past.

Oberon, rock the ground whereon these sleepers be

In Michigan, Oberon slips away after Labor Day,
the wheat beer with the sunny label sinks
from shelves, no sign of our king for months.

How long within this wood intend you stay?

Oberon returns in early spring, as days warm
and nights still dip below freezing. The buzz
of midnight tappings and release parties
awakens the Great Lakes State from slumber.

We bundle up and pour into Big Bear Lodge,
One Eyed Betty's, and Buck Shots Bar & Grille.
From Bad Axe to Detroit, Traverse City to
Kalamazoo, we witness our wheat king rising,
bright and citrusy. Oberon speaks to us.

Am not I thy lord? Throw down thy mittens!

Our bare hands cup Oberon's golden body,
hopping with hints of spice, an orange wedge
of mischief perched on the lip of summer.

We lean in close and toast. We've survived
another winter. We've survived each other.
Oh, the tales we have to tell.

My Oberon! What visions have I seen!

At long last, summer.

A Bad Feminist Reads the Bible

Literally, right from the beginning
there is only   the Word
and then only 11 women speaking,
their voices drowned
in a sea of shouts by 50 men.

The trend continues. In total,
49 named women speak. Whether
on papyrus, parchment, or palm leaves
women's words take up little space—
only one percent, the rest scrolled away.

Is it a righteous act to point out men
birthed the Bible? The good news
is that women shoved off the pages
pushed forth. Their songs and stories,
still being written.

Only a few read the Bible.
Some skim, tire, then toss aside.
Others read like children, command
the crust be cut away and eat only
the soft insides.

You don't have to walk far to find
full sentence women at the wells.
Drink deeply from this sacred source.
Admit hunger. Take in the morsels
crumpled near curbs, fragments

of the fleeting. Take it all in.
Lift your fallen selves and receive
these women who shall be read:
the ripped, the broken,
the glowing.

God of Plum and Thistle

Slip inside Mrs. Baron's second grade classroom
and children could be mistaken for angels,
legs and arms swept out from their sides; they lay
in a dazzling array, only a thin sheet of butcher paper
between their bodies and the cold floor.

Thanks to your partner, you have an outline, the teacher says.
It's up to you to fill it in. Pick your crayons and get busy.

Silence now, except for the sound of scribbling,
God of Soft Touch and Pressing Hard fills the room.
This is holy work, the traced and tracer working side by side
having taken turns to kneel next to the door of You.
Crayons praise every curve and sing:

Together, we are midwives of great works. I see you!
Take hold of my Hot Magenta hands, fall into these
Granny Smith Apple arms, and rest your head on my
Burnt Umber shoulder. Look around, we are building
a town filled with Forest Green and Mountain Meadow.

A bell rings.
School is over.

Oh, God of Inside and Outside the Lines, what now?
What now as we wander into your Wild Blue Yonder
with Jazzberry Jam hips and run through hot streets
on legs of Raw Sienna, our Dandelion hair
blowing in the wind?

Acknowledgements & Notes

I'm grateful to the editors of the publications in which the following poems first appeared:

Pilgrimage Magazine, "Storming Versailles."

Cardinal Sins, "Fourth Grade Place Settings."

Voices from the Porch (Main Street Rag), "Overture to the Porch on Crane Avenue."

Failbetter, "A Concise History of Michigan Cartology."

Windhover, "Having Bought St. Joseph, I Bury Him," "Grieving the God of My Youth" (part I), and "I Want a Church." "Grieving the God of My Youth" and "I Want a Church" also previously appeared in *Necessary Clearings*, published by Shabda Press.

Nude Bruce Review, "The Trouble with Reading in Your Hometown."

The Absence of Something Specified: an anthology (Fern Rock Falls, Noah's Shoes, Uttered Chaos, & Tiger's Eye Press), "Like the Parents They Never Knew."

The MOON magazine, "Castaways."

The Midwest Quarterly, "Maestro."

Poemeleon, "Word Whoreder."

Nimrod, "Searching."

Asylum Magazine, "Lists."

Zombies for a Cure (Electrik Milkbath Press), "Zombie Mommy."

Longest Hours: Thoughts While Waiting (Silver Boomer Books), "Waiting and Entering."

Harmony, "Autotomy, Self-Amputation."

To Unsnare Time's Warp: Stories and Poems about Dogs (Main Street Rag), "Sending the Dogs Off."

Women's Studies Quarterly, "They played Brady Bunch on Saturdays."

Crab Creek Review, "How to Become a Virgin" and "Protecting the Boys."

Encore Magazine, "If You Could Stand on Saturn."

Slipstream Magazine, "Magnetic Findings in the Czech Republic."

Full, an anthology of moon poems (Two Cups Press), "What We Don't Tell Our School Volunteers."

Thema Literary Journal ("Who Keeps it Tidy" issue), "Upon Reading the Settlement Agreement in Re: to Lyondell Chemical Company, *et al.,.*"

Ecotone, "Obsession #248: Moths."

[Ex]tinction & [Ex]tinguished: An Anthology of Things That No Longer Exist (Twelve Winters Press), "Longing for the Dynamite Days."

"She Stops Seeing Her Beauty at Age Seven" was inspired by Lorna Simpson's "Time Piece 1990."

In "Oberon, rock the ground whereon these sleepers be," the poem's title and italicized lines (with exception of "Throw down thy mittens!") are taken from William Shakespeare's *A Midsummer Night's Dream*. Larry Bell played the role of Oberon when his sixth grade class performed the play. He grew up and founded Bell's Brewery, which makes Oberon. If you live in warmer regions of the United States, like Florida, Arizona, and Puerto Rico, you can drink Oberon all year round.

A shout out to all the Dawgs for offering wisdom and encouragement.

Thanks to Donna Carroll, who read some of the earliest versions of this book.

A special thanks to John and Tom. Your love sustains me.

About the Author

Jennifer Clark is the author of two previous full-length poetry collections: *Johnny Appleseed: The Slice and Times of John Chapman* and *Necessary Clearings* (both published by Shabda Press). She is also the co-editor of the anthology, *Immigrations & Justice For Our Neighbors* (Celery City Books). Her poems, essays, and fiction have appeared in *Women's Studies Quarterly, Fiction Fix, Columbia Journal, Concho River Review, Ecotone,* and *Flyway,* among others. She lives in Kalamazoo, Michigan with her husband John and son Tom.

About the Press

UNSOLICITED PRESS is a small press in Portland, Oregon. Founded in 2012, the company publishes exceptional fiction, poetry, and creative nonfiction. Learn more at www.unsolicitedpress.com.

www.ingramcontent.com/pod-product-compliance
Lightning Source LLC
Chambersburg PA
CBHW030120100526
44591CB00009B/473